I0016992

About the Author

With over two decades of immersive experience in the realm of cybersecurity, the author's distinguished background in Communications and IT, honed during a commendable military career in the UK Armed Forces, serves as a robust foundation for their insights in this critical field. Their unique perspective, coupled with expertise in developing and implementing comprehensive security controls, not only enhances their credibility but also resonates deeply with those seeking to navigate the complexities of digital security today. Through this book, they aim to empower readers by demystifying cybersecurity and its vital role in today's interconnected world.

The author has dedicated more than 20 years to safeguarding organizations from ever-evolving cyber threats, showcasing their proficiency across various sectors, including collaboration with local and central government departments in the UK. By seamlessly integrating military discipline with industry expertise, they have developed a pragmatic approach to cybersecurity that balances operational needs with strategic insight. Their contributions have been pivotal in implementing robust security frameworks that protect sensitive information and maintain trust in digital environments.

Educationally, the author combines formal training with real-world experience, which shapes their writing and thought processes. Their journey as a writer began as they sought to share the critical lessons learned from practical engagements in the field. Inspired by the urgency of raising awareness about cybersecurity, they embraced the pen as a tool to educate and inspire a broader audience. With a focus on making complex topics accessible, their writing style is characterized by clarity and engagement, aimed at demystifying cybersecurity concepts for all readers.

Passionate about knowledge sharing, the author believes in the importance of relatable communication. They strive to present intricate subjects in a manner that is not only understandable but also engaging for diverse audiences. By leveraging their personal experiences and professional insights, they create content that resonates and inspires action. Their commitment to fostering a culture of cybersecurity awareness and resilience makes their contributions invaluable in the contemporary digital landscape.

Driven by a mission to illuminate the critical importance of cybersecurity, the author aspires to continue educating and engaging with audiences through various mediums. Looking ahead, they aim to expand their reach, empowering more individuals and organizations to recognize and counteract cyber threats effectively. With a goal of fostering a more secure digital future, they hope to inspire a generation of cybersecurity professionals and enthusiasts who will champion safety in the cyberspace.

Table of Contents

Chapter 1: Introduction to Cyber Security Operations

Chapter 2: Incident Response Fundamentals

Chapter 3: Security Information and Event Management (SIEM)

Chapter 4: Security Operations Center's (SOC)

Chapter 5: Threat Detection Mechanisms

Chapter 6: Tools and Technologies in Cyber Security Operations

Chapter 7: Incident Handling Procedures

Chapter 8: Digital Forensics in Cyber Security

Chapter 9: Compliance and Regulatory Frameworks

(1) - 9.1 Overview of Cyber Security Regulations

(2) - 9.2 Compliance Standards (e.g., GDPR, HIPAA)

(3) - 9.3 Risk Management and Compliance Strategies

Chapter 10: Threat Hunting Strategies

(1) - 10.1 Definition and Importance of Threat Hunting

(2) - 10.2 Threat Hunting Methodologies

(3) - 10.3 Tools and Resources for Threat Hunting

Chapter 11: Incident Response Plans and Policies

Chapter 12: Cyber Security Metrics and Reporting

Chapter 13: Advanced Persistent Threats (APTs)

Chapter 14: Vendor and Third-party Risk Management

(1) - 14.1 Assessing Third-party Cyber Risks

(2) - 14.2 Frameworks for Vendor Security Assessment

(3) - 14.3 Incident Response Coordination with Third-party Vendors

Chapter 15: Future Trends in Cyber Security Operations

(1) - 15.1 Emerging Threat Landscapes

(2) - 15.2 Innovations in Cyber Security Technologies

(3) - 15.3 Preparing for the Future of Cyber Security Operations

Chapter 1: Introduction to Cyber Security Operations

1.1 Overview of Cyber Security Operations

Cyber Security Operations is fundamentally about establishing a strategic and tactical framework for the management and protection of information assets. This expansive field encompasses all activities aimed at ensuring that sensitive data remains secure against an evolving landscape of threats. Organizations invest in Cyber Security Operations to create robust defenses that not only guard against unauthorized access but also mitigate risks inherent in today's digital environment. This involves implementing policies, processes, and technologies designed to safeguard essential information and ensure that, when faced with security challenges, a coordinated response is initiated. The interaction between strategy and tactics is crucial; while overarching strategies dictate the long-term vision for security, tactical operations are necessary to execute these strategies effectively on a day-to-day basis.

The role of Cyber Security Operations extends beyond mere defense; it is also crucial for preventing, detecting, and responding to security incidents. Preventive measures may include training staff on best practices and deploying advanced technologies that can identify and neutralize threats before they escalate. Detection mechanisms are equally vital, encompassing tools such as Security Information and Event Management (SIEM) systems that monitor network activity for anomalies. When incidents occur, a swift and effective response is essential. This response may involve incident investigation procedures that not only address the immediate situation but also apply lessons learned to improve future security posture. Ultimately, successful Cyber Security Operations create a resilient environment where organizations can navigate their digital landscapes with confidence.

Engaging in continuous assessment and improvement of Cyber Security Operations is critical. Organizations should constantly analyze their security frameworks and remain adaptable to the rapidly changing threat landscape. By fostering a culture of proactive security awareness and ensuring that all personnel are equipped with the knowledge to recognize potential threats, companies can bolster their defenses remarkably. Establishing clear communication protocols for incident response teams ensures that responsibilities are understood and that actions are coordinated effectively, enhancing the organization's overall resilience against cyber threats.

1.2 Importance of Cyber Security in Modern Organizations

Cybersecurity plays a crucial role in protecting sensitive information and ensuring the operational integrity of modern organizations. In an age where data breaches and cyberattacks are increasingly common, the ability to safeguard confidential information from unauthorized access is paramount. Sensitive data, such as personal information, financial records, and intellectual property, can be the lifeblood of an organization. When this information is compromised, the repercussions can be dire. Organizations must implement robust cybersecurity measures to not only protect this information but also to maintain trust with clients and stakeholders. A breach can lead to a loss of operational integrity, disrupting services and potentially compromising the organization's ability to function effectively.

The financial and reputational impacts of cyber threats cannot be overstated. Organizations infected by ransomware or subject to data breaches often face hefty financial penalties, remediation costs, and legal liabilities. For instance, the costs associated with recovery, including system repairs, data restoration, and potential compensation payouts to affected individuals, can escalate quickly. Moreover, the reputational damage incurred from a cyber incident can take years to repair. Customers may lose faith in a company's ability to protect their data, leading to a decline in sales and market share. In addition to financial losses, organizations must navigate the complex landscape of public perception and regulatory scrutiny following a cyber incident. This underscores the need for comprehensive cybersecurity strategies that not only address immediate threats but also foster a long-term culture of security awareness and resilience.

Proactively implementing cybersecurity measures is not just a reactive approach; it is a vital investment in the future of an organization. By fostering a culture of cybersecurity awareness and integrating security protocols into every aspect of the business, organizations can dramatically reduce their risk exposure. Regular training sessions for employees, investment in advanced security technologies, and the establishment of incident response teams are essential steps in building a resilient security posture. When organizations prioritize cybersecurity, they not only shield themselves from potential threats but also position themselves as trustworthy entities in the marketplace, ultimately leading to greater business success and stability.

1.3 Evolution of Cyber Security Practices

The historical development of cyber security practices can be traced back to the early days of computing when the primary focus was on protecting physical assets and ensuring basic system integrity. Initially, this involved straightforward measures such as password protection, access controls, and simple firewalls designed to prevent unauthorized access. As technology advanced, so did the sophistication of cyber threats, leading to the creation of a more complex security landscape. The introduction of viruses and worms in the late 1980s prompted the need for antivirus software, marking a significant shift in how organizations approached their security strategies. Subsequent decades saw the rise of the internet, which opened new avenues for cybercrime, and prompted security professionals to develop policies and practices to address increasingly complex threats, such as phishing and denial-of-service attacks. This historical trajectory laid the groundwork for the multi-layered defense strategies organizations use today, integrating not only technical solutions but also comprehensive risk management and compliance frameworks.

The evolution of cyber defense strategies has been significantly shaped by emerging technologies. Advancements such as cloud computing, mobile devices, and the Internet of Things (IoT) have transformed the threat landscape and influenced how organizations implement security measures. For instance, the shift to cloud services required a re-evaluation of traditional security models, leading to the development of practices such as secure API design, data encryption in transit, and continuous monitoring of cloud environments. Similarly, the proliferation of IoT devices has introduced new vulnerabilities, necessitating innovative approaches to network security and device authentication. As machine learning and artificial intelligence technologies become more prevalent, they are being leveraged to enhance threat detection and automate response efforts. This dynamic interplay between technology and cyber security practices emphasizes the need for security operations teams to stay informed and agile in order to effectively combat evolving threats and safeguard critical assets.

To stay ahead in this expanding and shifting landscape of cyber security, professionals must continually update their knowledge and skills. Engaging in ongoing training and staying informed about the latest trends and technologies can provide valuable insights into best practices for enhancing security posture. Implementing a culture of security awareness within organizations can further fortify defenses as employees become the first line of protection against cyber threats.

Chapter 2: Incident Response Fundamentals

2.1 Definition and Objectives of Incident Response

Incident response refers to the systematic approach taken by organizations to prepare for, detect, respond to, and recover from security breaches and vulnerabilities that may compromise sensitive data and disrupt operations. The primary objectives of incident response are to identify the breach swiftly, contain the impact, eradicate the threat, and recover from the incident with minimal disruption. By implementing a well-structured incident response plan, organizations not only mitigate the immediate threats but also enhance their overall security posture. This involves understanding the nature of potential incidents, the tactics employed by cybercriminals, and the vulnerabilities that could be exploited within the organization's systems.

A swift and effective incident response is crucial in minimizing damage and restoring normal operations. When an incident occurs, every second counts. The longer it takes to detect and respond to a security breach, the greater the potential for damage, including data loss, financial repercussions, and damage to an organization's reputation. An effective response enables organizations to quickly isolate affected systems, thereby limiting the spread of the incident. Additionally, timely communication with stakeholders, including employees, customers, and regulatory bodies, is essential during these events to maintain trust and transparency. By fostering a culture that prioritizes incident response, organizations can ensure that they are better prepared to handle incidents when they arise, thus reducing recovery time and costs while preserving business continuity.

Ultimately, developing a robust incident response capability is not merely about managing emergencies but is a proactive strategy that reinforces organizational resilience. Organizations should regularly test and update their incident response plans, ensuring that all personnel are familiar with their roles in an incident scenario. Investing in training and simulations helps prepare teams to react efficiently, making the response not only quicker but more effective. Additionally, leveraging threat intelligence can significantly enhance an organization's ability to anticipate and respond to incidents before they escalate.

2.2 Incident Response Lifecycle

The Incident Response Lifecycle consists of several critical stages that provide a structured approach to handling security incidents effectively. The first stage, preparation, is essential for establishing the foundation upon which all other stages rest. This involves developing incident response policies, training staff, and ensuring that the necessary tools and resources are in place. Organizations must conduct regular risk assessments and create a well-documented plan that enables quick and effective responses to potential threats. In the detection stage, continuous monitoring of systems and networks helps identify anomalies and potential incidents as early as possible. Effective use of Security Information and Event Management (SIEM) tools can be instrumental here, enabling teams to spot unusual activities indicative of a breach. The analysis stage involves a thorough investigation of the incident to understand its nature and scope. This requires examining logs, gathering forensic evidence, and sometimes even engaging external experts to identify the attackers' tactics, techniques, and procedures. Once the analysis provides a clear picture, the containment stage kicks in, aiming to restrict the threat's spread and minimize damage. Containment strategies can vary from isolating affected systems to implementing temporary measures that allow operations to continue safely. After containment is achieved, the eradication stage focuses on removing the threat from the environment. This could involve deleting malware, applying patches, or even re-imaging affected systems to ensure that the threat is entirely eliminated. The final stage is recovery, where efforts shift to restoring systems and services to normal operation while ensuring that the vulnerabilities exploited during the incident are adequately addressed to prevent reoccurrence. This stage may also involve continuous monitoring to ensure that no remnants of the incident persist. Each stage of the Incident Response Lifecycle is crucial for achieving effective incident management outcomes. Preparation ensures that organizations are well-equipped to handle incidents, while detection and analysis allow for timely responses. Containment and eradication minimize the impact of threats, and recovery brings systems back online securely. Recognizing the significance of each stage helps organizations appreciate the interconnected nature of incident response. Preparation without effective detection can lead to missed incidents, while analysis without proper containment measures can exacerbate potential damage. By focusing on a holistic approach to the Incident Response Lifecycle, organizations can significantly enhance their security posture, ensuring they are not only quick to respond but also resilient in the face of evolving threats. For practical implementation, regular drills and tabletop exercises can help reinforce these stages, allowing SOC teams to practice their responses and refine their processes in a controlled environment.

2.3 Key Roles and Responsibilities

The incident response team plays a crucial role in safeguarding an organization against cyber threats, and understanding the primary roles within this team is essential for effective incident management. The Incident Response Manager leads the team, overseeing the entire incident handling process and ensuring that communication flows smoothly among team members and stakeholders. They are responsible for establishing protocols and ensuring the team is prepared to respond to incidents swiftly and effectively.

Alongside the manager is the Forensic Analyst, whose primary responsibility is to investigate incidents, analyze the evidence, and determine the nature and extent of the attack. They work closely with the Threat Intelligence Analyst, who gathers and analyzes threat data to identify potential attacks and assesses vulnerabilities within the organization. The Security Engineer is vital in implementing security measures and ensuring that any vulnerabilities in systems or networks are patched and fortified against potential exploitation. Each team member must clearly understand their responsibilities and work cohesively to ensure a timely response to incidents.

Collaboration among incident response team members significantly enhances the effectiveness of incident response efforts. When each team member actively shares insights and expertise, the collective knowledge creates a more robust response strategy. For instance, the interplay between forensic analysis and threat intelligence can reveal patterns that inform preventive measures for future incidents. Regular drills and tabletop exercises foster strong communication, ensuring that team members understand their roles and how they interdepend. This synergy reduces response time and increases the overall resilience of the organization against cyber threats. It is essential for teams to cultivate a culture of collaboration, where open lines of communication and shared objectives lead to more effective incident mitigation.

Teams can greatly benefit from establishing clear communication channels, utilizing shared platforms where all relevant data can be accessed in real-time. This not only streamlines the response during an actual incident but also helps in refining incident management protocols continually. By adopting a forward-thinking approach that leverages both technology and teamwork, incident response teams can ensure they are always one step ahead in an ever-evolving threat landscape.

Chapter 3: Security Information and Event Management (SIEM)

3.1 What is SIEM?

Security Information and Event Management, commonly referred to as SIEM, is a critical framework utilized by organizations to gather, analyze, and manage security data from across their digital infrastructure. Its primary purpose lies in the aggregation of vast amounts of security-related information from various sources such as servers, network devices, domain controllers, and other security solutions. SIEM systems process and correlate this data in real-time, providing a comprehensive view of security events and incidents. By consolidating information into a centralized platform, SIEM enables organizations to respond more effectively to threats, while also assisting in compliance with regulatory requirements. The ability to analyze historical and real-time data enhances an organization's capacity to detect anomalies and respond promptly to security incidents, transforming raw data into actionable intelligence.

The role of SIEM in improving visibility across an organization's security landscape is profound. By deploying SIEM, security teams gain a holistic view of their environment, enabling them to monitor activities occurring in real time. This heightened visibility is crucial for identifying potential threats before they can escalate into significant breaches. SIEM not only aggregates logs and alerts from multiple security sources but also enriches this data with contextual information to analyze patterns and trends over time. This form of analysis allows Security Operations Centre's (SOCs) to prioritize incidents based on severity and potential impact, leading to more efficient incident response. Ultimately, SIEM strengthens an organization's security posture by providing a clear, concise, and comprehensive overview of security activities, which is essential for fast-paced environments where timely decision-making can mitigate risks and protect critical assets.

For organizations aiming to enhance their threat detection capabilities, deploying a SIEM solution is a fundamental step. Engaging with the available features in a SIEM tool, such as custom alerting and playbook automation, can significantly optimize response times to incidents. Ensure to regularly review and update your SIEM configurations and rules, as evolving threats often require adjustments in monitoring strategies. Investing in ongoing training for your SOC team to effectively utilize the SIEM system can further bolster your organization's defenses against emerging security challenges.

3.2 Components of a SIEM Solution

SIEM solutions are essential in the realm of cybersecurity, functioning as the backbone of threat detection and incident response. The fundamental components of these solutions include data collection, normalization, analysis, and reporting. Data collection involves aggregating logs and events from various sources within the organization's infrastructure, such as firewalls, servers, applications, and endpoints. This stage is critical as it sets the stage for the remaining processes. Following collection, normalization takes place, converting disparate data formats into a consistent structure that allows for easier analysis. Through normalization, SIEM systems can efficiently correlate data and identify patterns or anomalies that may indicate security threats.

Once the data is normalized, the analysis phase begins. Advanced algorithms and analytics tools sift through the structured data to uncover potentially malicious activities. This part of the process often employs machine learning techniques to improve detection rates and reduce false positives. Finally, reporting is crucial for translating the insights gained during analysis into actionable intelligence for security teams. Effective reporting provides context and clarity, allowing security operations centre's (SOCs) to respond swiftly and decisively to incidents.

Integrating multiple data sources into a cohesive SIEM architecture is paramount for enhancing security posture. A robust SIEM solution leverages holistic visibility across the organization by collecting data from various points, including cloud services, on-premise appliances, and third-party applications. This integration enables security teams to correlate events from different sources, constructing a more comprehensive picture of existing vulnerabilities and potential threats. Without this multifaceted view, cyber incidents could go unnoticed or be misinterpreted, leading to ineffective responses. Ensuring that your SIEM solution can seamlessly integrate with diverse data sources, such as threat intelligence feeds and external security services, enhances threat detection capabilities and empowers organizations to thwart attacks proactively. Always remember that the strength of your SIEM solution lies in its ability to bring together varied data into a unified framework, amplifying your overall security effectiveness.

3.3 Best Practices for SIEM Implementation

Effective SIEM deployment starts with defining clear objectives and scope. Organizations must identify the specific goals they aim to achieve with their SIEM solution. This could range from regulatory compliance, threat detection to operational efficiency. Next, it is crucial to outline the scope of data that the SIEM will analyze. This involves selecting which log sources and security events to monitor. By doing this, teams can focus their efforts on the most relevant data, thus improving the accuracy of threat detection. Taking the time to draft a well-defined deployment strategy significantly enhances the chances of successful integration of the SIEM into existing security ecosystems. Additionally, involving key stakeholders during the planning phase ensures alignment on project objectives and resource allocation, paving the way for a smoother implementation process.

Continuous monitoring and regular updates serve as essential practices to enhance SIEM performance. Security threats are constantly evolving, making it vital for organizations to maintain a proactive stance. Implementing real-time monitoring allows security teams to respond immediately to suspicious activities, thus minimizing potential damage. Along with live monitoring, regularly updating the SIEM software and threat intelligence feeds plays a critical role in keeping the system effective against emerging threats. Moreover, routine assessments and performance tuning help identify gaps that may arise due to changes in the IT environment or security landscape. Organizations should establish scheduled review processes to assess the effectiveness of their SIEM, ensuring that it adapts to new threats and operational changes over time. Strong collaboration between SOC teams and threat intelligence sources can facilitate robust updates, enabling security architectures to stay a step ahead of adversaries.

Establishing a SIEM that leverages ongoing refinement and strategic planning truly enhances its effectiveness. Continuous improvement should be viewed as a core component of the SIEM deployment strategy, emphasizing the necessity of adapting to the ever-changing security environment.

Chapter 4: Security Operations Center's (SOC)

4.1 SOC Structure and Functionality

The organizational structure of a Security Operations Centre (SOC) is pivotal for effectively managing security operations. Typically, a SOC is composed of various specialized teams that focus on aspects such as threat detection, incident response, and compliance management. At the helm is the SOC manager who oversees the daily operations, ensuring that the team is coordinating well and objectives are being met. Beneath the manager, you will often find tiered levels of analysts. Tier 1 analysts are responsible for initial monitoring and triaging of alerts, acting as the first line of defense. Tier 2 analysts delve deeper into complex alerts, conducting investigations to determine if they represent real threats. Finally, Tier 3 analysts or incident responders handle the most sophisticated incidents, utilizing advanced skills to mitigate threats, analyze malware, and restore systems. This structured approach allows SOC teams to operate efficiently, fostering a streamlined workflow that enhances overall security posture.

Supporting the operational capabilities of a SOC are various technologies and processes tailored to bolster its effectiveness. Central to these capabilities is a Security Information and Event Management (SIEM) system, which aggregates and analyzes data from diverse sources. By correlating logs and alarms, a SIEM enables teams to identify potential security incidents in real-time, facilitating a proactive response. Alongside SIEM, other vital technologies include intrusion detection systems (IDS), threat intelligence platforms, and endpoint detection and response (EDR) solutions. These tools work in harmony, creating a robust security framework that empowers analysts to quickly detect, investigate, and respond to threats. Processes play an equally critical role; established workflows for incident response ensure that when an alert is triggered, the SOC knows precisely how to engage. This may encompass predefined playbooks that dictate the response steps, communication protocols, and timing of actions. Together, these technologies and processes form the backbone of a SOC's operational capability, allowing teams to efficiently manage and mitigate threats.

A practical tip for SOC teams is to regularly review and practice incident response playbooks. Engaging in tabletop exercises and simulations not only enhances familiarity with protocols but also fosters collaboration among team members. This preparation ensures that when a real incident occurs, the SOC can respond swiftly and effectively, minimizing damage and improving recovery times. Consider incorporating feedback mechanisms to continually update and refine these playbooks based on lessons learned from previous incidents.

4.2 Types of SOCs: In-house vs Outsourced

In-house Security Operations Center's (SOCs) and outsourced SOC models serve the same primary purpose of safeguarding an organization's information and assets, but they differ in structure, operation, and resource allocation. An in-house SOC is established within the organization, involving employees who work directly for the company and have intimate knowledge of its specific security needs, culture, and operational frameworks. This familiarity can enhance the efficiency of threat detection and response, allowing for tailored solutions that align closely with the organization's objectives. Additionally, in-house teams often benefit from a higher level of control over security policies, response times, and alignment with internal processes. However, the challenges include substantial costs in hiring, training, and maintaining a skilled workforce, ongoing investments in technology and infrastructure, and the potential for knowledge silos that may develop within a confined team. In contrast, outsourced SOCs leverage the expertise and resources of third-party vendors who specialize in security operations. Outsourcing can provide access to a wider array of skills and technologies that may not be readily attainable otherwise, along with cost efficiency because organizations can avoid the upfront expenditures associated with building and maintaining an in-house team. Nonetheless, the drawbacks often lie in the potential lack of integration and communication between the outsourced team and the internal staff, resulting in misalignment and slower response times. Moreover, organizations might feel uneasy entrusting sensitive information to external parties, raising concerns about data privacy and compliance with regulations.

Organizations contemplating the choice between in-house and outsourced SOCs should consider several important factors. The level of security expertise within the organization can greatly influence the decision; if sufficient in-house knowledge exists, an organization might lean toward developing an in-house SOC to maintain control and foster a culture of cybersecurity. In contrast, if the organization lacks resources or expertise, outsourcing may be the most viable option. Another factor includes the organization's size, budget, and specific needs. Larger organizations might benefit from in-house SOCs due to their capacity to hire and sustain security professionals, while smaller entities might find that outsourcing provides necessary security services without the significant investment. Moreover, regulatory and compliance requirements also play a crucial role in the decision-making process. Organizations handling sensitive data often require a higher level of scrutiny and might prefer in-house operations to ensure strict compliance. Additionally, the scalability of services is another important consideration; organizations anticipating growth may favour outsourced SOCs that can quickly adjust to increasing security demands without the complexities of managing a larger internal workforce. Ultimately, aligning the choice of SOC model with the organization's strategic goals and risk tolerance is essential for effective security operations.

When evaluating SOC structures, organizations should also keep in mind the importance of blending expertise with technology. Whether opting for in-house or outsourced solutions, establishing a collaborative approach that leverages the strengths of both models can lead to better overall security posture. Engaging with third-party vendors doesn't mean relinquishing control; organizations can create partnerships where both internal and external resources unify their efforts in a cohesive manner. This hybrid approach encourages knowledge sharing and enhances incident response capabilities, providing organizations with the agility to adapt in a constantly evolving threat landscape. Assessing the complexity of the security challenges faced can provide insight into which model best suits the needs of the organization, allowing for an informed decision that ultimately bolsters the overall security strategy.

4.3 Measuring SOC Effectiveness

Measurement metrics are crucial for assessing the effectiveness of Security Operations Center (SOC) operations. Various metrics can be employed to evaluate how well a SOC performs and its impact on the organization's security posture. Commonly used metrics include mean time to detect (MTTD) and mean time to respond (MTTR), which provide insights into how quickly threats are identified and addressed. Additionally, the number of incidents detected by the SOC, along with the percentage of false positives, helps to gauge the accuracy and efficiency of monitoring tools and methodologies in place. These metrics should ideally align with organizational goals, ensuring that the SOC's performance supports broader security objectives. Moreover, the frequency and severity of security incidents can also indicate the maturity and resilience of SOC operations, enabling teams to make informed adjustments to tactics and strategy. Integrating these KPIs into regular reporting can make it easier for stakeholders to understand the SOC's value proposition and reinforce its role in safeguarding organizational assets.

Understanding the relationship between SOC performance and the overall organizational security posture is a vital aspect of measuring effectiveness. A well-functioning SOC should ultimately lead to improved organizational resilience against cyber threats. For example, a responsive SOC can minimize the impact of breaches by enabling swift incident response and recovery, thereby reducing recovery time and costs associated with security incidents. Furthermore, there is a strong correlation between proactive threat detection capabilities and the overall security posture. When a SOC excels at identifying threats early, it helps organizations avoid potential breaches before they escalate. Additionally, ongoing training and skill development within the SOC enhance the capacity to adapt to emerging threats, which is essential for maintaining security over time. This adaptive nature influences the organization's risk management strategy and bolsters confidence in digital operations among internal and external stakeholders.

Ultimately, measuring SOC effectiveness is not just about numbers; it reflects the SOC's ability to contribute to comprehensive security strategies. Organizations should focus on establishing a robust framework for evaluating these performance metrics that aligns with their specific security needs and threats landscape. Emphasizing continual improvement and the adoption of best practices will create a culture of security within the SOC that resonates throughout the entire organization. A practical approach is to regularly review and refine these metrics in collaboration with business units, ensuring they accurately capture the evolving threat landscape, and adjust the SOC's focus accordingly.

Chapter 5: Threat Detection Mechanisms

5.1 Types of Cyber Threats

Cyber threats can be broadly categorized into several types, each posing unique risks and challenges to organizations. Malware is perhaps the most well-known of these threats. It refers to malicious software designed to disrupt, damage, or gain unauthorized access to computer systems. This category includes viruses, worms, Trojans, ransomware, and spyware. Each type of malware operates differently, with some designed for specific targets while others spread rapidly across networks. Phishing is another prevalent type of cyber threat. This tactic often involves deceptive emails or messages from seemingly legitimate sources aimed at tricking users into divulging sensitive information, such as passwords or financial details. Phishing attacks have become increasingly sophisticated, with attackers using social engineering techniques to tailor their messages to specific individuals or organizations. Advanced Persistent Threats (APTs) represent a more complex and targeted category of cyber threat. These threats involve prolonged and targeted attacks where infiltrators gain access to a network and remain undetected for extended periods. APTs often aim to steal sensitive data or espionage, making them particularly concerning for large organizations and government entities.

The nature of cyber threats is constantly evolving, necessitating adaptive detection approaches to combat them effectively. Attackers are continually developing new techniques and strategies to bypass existing security measures. This dynamic landscape means that traditional reactive defense mechanisms are often insufficient. Security professionals must employ proactive measures, incorporating threat intelligence to stay updated on emerging threats and vulnerabilities. Adaptive detection relies on machine learning and behavioural analysis to identify unusual patterns or activities that may indicate a threat, significantly enhancing the chances of early detection. As cyber threats continue to grow in complexity, organizations must foster a culture of continuous learning and agile response. This includes regular updates to security protocols, ongoing training for personnel, and the implementation of advanced security solutions capable of evolving alongside the threat landscape.

Staying informed about the specific types of cyber threats relevant to your organization is crucial for developing an effective security posture. Regularly reviewing threat intelligence reports and engaging with industry communities can provide valuable insights into the tactics employed by cybercriminals. By understanding the nuances of threats like malware, phishing, and APTs, security teams, incident response units, and SOC teams can ensure they are adequately prepared and equipped to defend against these evolving challenges.

5.2 Technologies for Threat Detection

A broad range of technologies exists to enhance cyber threat detection, each with its own mechanisms and methodologies. Anomaly detection, for instance, relies on identifying deviations from established patterns of behaviour, which can signal potential threats. By establishing a baseline of normal activity within the network, anomaly detection systems scrutinize data flows to recognize unusual patterns that may indicate a security breach.

Behavioural analytics complements this approach by assessing user behaviour and device interactions to spot inconsistencies that may suggest insider threats or compromised accounts. This technology leverages historical data to understand typical user activities, allowing it to spot irregular actions that deviate from the norm. Together, these technologies can serve as early warning systems, enabling organizations to respond swiftly to potential incidents before they evolve into significant breaches.

The effectiveness of detection technologies can vary widely based on the specific threat scenarios encountered. For example, while anomaly detection may excel in detecting sophisticated attacks like Advanced Persistent Threats (APTs), it can generate false positives in different contexts, leading to alert fatigue among security teams. Behavioural analytics often provides a more nuanced view, effectively identifying threats that arise from legitimate users due to compromised credentials or malicious insiders. However, depending on the organization's environment and the quality of the data being analyzed, the impact of these technologies can differ. In environments with high user mobility and diverse devices, correct implementation becomes paramount, as high variability can obscure meaningful insights. Therefore, a blended approach—utilizing multiple detection technologies tailored to the specific security posture and threat landscape of the organization—often yields the most effective results.

Staying informed about evolving technologies and their respective effectiveness in threat detection scenarios is essential for security operations teams. Continuous monitoring and adaptable strategies, along with regular assessments of existing tools, can significantly enhance incident response capabilities. It's beneficial for organizations to regularly evaluate the performance of their detection technologies against the latest attack vectors to ensure they remain effective. Integrating threat intelligence feeds into detection systems can also sharpen their focus, enabling them to adapt and respond to new types of threats as they become identified in the broader threat landscape.

5.3 Threat Intelligence Integration

Integrating threat intelligence into existing security frameworks is essential for creating a proactive defense posture. This integration allows security teams to stay ahead of evolving threats, transform raw data into actionable insights, and enhance their ability to respond swiftly to potential incidents. With proper integration, organizations can diminish response times, enabling teams to anticipate attacks rather than merely react to them. Threat intelligence provides critical context around the nature of emerging threats, including the tactics, techniques, and procedures (TTPs) employed by cyber adversaries. By incorporating this intelligence into their security frameworks, organizations create a dynamic security landscape that adapts and evolves in response to new information, ultimately leading to a stronger defense against sophisticated attacks.

Leveraging threat intelligence feeds enhances detection capabilities by enriching existing security data with contextual information. Security information and event management (SIEM) systems can integrate these feeds to provide enriched alerts, helping analysts differentiate between benign activities and actual threats. This approach allows for more accurate correlation of security events, giving SOC teams better visibility into potential incidents. Automated tools can sift through vast amounts of data, identifying patterns and anomalies that might otherwise go unnoticed. By utilizing these feeds, organizations can prioritize remediation efforts, focusing on the most significant threats and vulnerabilities. Furthermore, threat intelligence can help in developing threat models tailored to specific environments, ensuring that detection measures are both relevant and effective.

For organizations seeking to implement threat intelligence effectively, it is crucial to establish a feedback loop. Regularly updating and reviewing the threat intelligence integration process will ensure that the security posture remains aligned with changing threat landscapes. Collaborating with third-party suppliers who offer expert intelligence and solutions can further enhance a security operation's capabilities. Engaging in threat intelligence sharing communities can foster knowledge exchange, leading to improved threat detection and defense strategies. Adopting these practices can significantly bolster an organization's ability to proactively defend against cyber threats.

Chapter 6: Tools and Technologies in Cyber Security Operations

6.1 Overview of Cyber Security Tools

Cyber security tools are critical assets in protecting an organization's digital infrastructure. Among the most essential tools are firewalls and intrusion detection systems (IDS). Firewalls serve as the first line of defense, controlling the incoming and outgoing network traffic based on predetermined security rules. They act as barriers between trusted internal networks and untrusted external networks, filtering data packets to prevent unauthorized access and attacks. Different types of firewalls, such as packet-filtering firewalls, stateful inspection firewalls, and next-generation firewalls, cater to various security needs, offering different levels of security and performance. On the other hand, intrusion detection systems monitor and analyze network traffic for suspicious activities or policy violations. They can be classified as network-based or host-based and employ both signature-based and anomaly-based detection techniques to identify threats in real time. Both firewalls and IDS are indispensable in detecting and mitigating potential security incidents, safeguarding sensitive data from a multitude of cyber threats.

In the broader security architecture of an organization, these tools play pivotal roles, integrating seamlessly with other components to enhance overall security posture. Firewalls and IDS are foundation elements in a multi-layered security strategy known as defense-in-depth. This strategy includes additional layers, such as endpoint protection, data encryption, and identity management systems. Each tool addresses distinct aspects of security; for instance, while firewalls focus on preventing unauthorized access, IDS concentrates on detecting and responding to intrusions once they occur. Moreover, Security Information and Event Management (SIEM) systems aggregate logs and alerts from various tools across the network, including firewalls and IDS, to provide a comprehensive view of an organization's security landscape. This layered approach not only increases visibility but also facilitates quicker incident response through coordinated efforts across all security components.

To enhance the efficacy of these security tools, continuous monitoring and regular updating are essential. Ensuring that firewalls and IDS are properly configured, regularly patched, and effectively integrated within the security architecture will significantly reduce an organization's risk exposure. Establishing a feedback loop with incident response teams can also help refine the rules and parameters for these tools, enabling them to adapt to new threats as they emerge. This proactive stance in maintaining cyber security tools can bolster an organization's defense mechanisms significantly.

6.2 Emerging Technologies in Cyber Security

Emerging technologies such as artificial intelligence (AI) and machine learning (ML) are significantly reshaping cyber security operations. These advancements enable organizations to analyze vast amounts of data in real time, allowing for quicker detection of anomalies that may indicate a security breach. AI algorithms can learn from previous incidents, adapting and improving their response strategies as they gather more data. This ability to predict and respond to threats with increased accuracy is one of the key benefits of integrating AI into security frameworks. Furthermore, tools powered by machine learning can automate mundane tasks, such as sorting through millions of log entries, freeing up cyber security professionals to focus on more complex challenges.

However, the adoption of these new technologies is not without its challenges. Integrating AI and ML into existing security infrastructures can require significant investment and expertise. Organizations may face difficulties in ensuring the quality of data inputs, as biased or inaccurate data can lead to ineffective threat detection. Additionally, as cyber attackers adopt sophisticated strategies, the AI systems designed to counter these threats must also evolve continuously. There is an ongoing race between defenders utilizing innovative technologies and adversaries leveraging the same or even more advanced tools. Furthermore, reliance on automated systems can create new vulnerabilities, as a single exploitation could potentially give attackers access to extensive systems and data.

A best practice for organizations considering the integration of these emerging technologies is to implement a hybrid approach. Combining human expertise with machine-driven capabilities can create a resilient security strategy that adapts to the ever-evolving landscape of cyber threats. By emphasizing ongoing training and awareness for staff, organizations can ensure that their teams leverage technological advancements effectively while remaining vigilant against new forms of attacks.

6.3 Tool Selection Criteria

When selecting security tools, organizations must consider several key criteria to ensure that the tools align with their unique needs and comply with relevant regulatory requirements. One important criterion is the tool's ability to integrate seamlessly with existing systems and workflows. Tools should fit within the organization's current architecture without causing significant disruption or requiring extensive training. Additionally, scalability is crucial; the selected tools must be able to grow with the organization's changing needs, whether due to increased data volume or changes in regulatory frameworks. Another vital factor is the comprehensiveness of the tool's features—an effective security tool should provide capabilities that address multiple aspects of security, from prevention and detection to incident response. Cost is also a pivotal consideration; organizations should evaluate not only the initial purchase price but also the total cost of ownership over the tool's lifecycle, including ongoing maintenance and support costs. Finally, organizations must assess the vendor's reputation and reliability, ensuring that the chosen provider offers robust support and regular updates that respond to the evolving threat landscape.

The process of selecting security tools must align closely with an organization's overall cybersecurity strategy. This alignment ensures that any tool chosen will not only provide tactical benefits but will also contribute to the strategic objectives of improving security posture and risk management. For instance, if an organization's strategy emphasizes proactive threat detection, then tools with advanced analytics and real-time monitoring capabilities should be prioritized. It's essential to involve key stakeholders from various departments, including IT, compliance, and risk management, in these discussions to ensure that the selected tools meet cross-functional needs and enable a uniform approach to cybersecurity. By maintaining this strategic alignment, organizations can enhance their resilience against cyber threats while ensuring compliance with regulatory standards.

An effective tip for organizations embarking on the tool selection journey is to conduct a thorough evaluation of potential tools through practical demonstrations or pilot programs. This hands-on experience allows teams to assess the usability and effectiveness of a tool in real-world scenarios. Engaging with community feedback, industry reviews, and case studies can provide insights into the tool's performance across different environments. Implementing a structured selection process that includes criteria based on organizational goals and strategies will not only facilitate effective decision-making but also foster a culture of continuous improvement in cybersecurity efforts.

Chapter 7: Incident Handling Procedures

7.1 Preparing for Incidents

Preparing for incidents in a cybersecurity context requires a systematic approach that begins with risk assessment and the establishment of robust security policies. Understanding potential threats and vulnerabilities is crucial for developing a layered defense strategy. This involves identifying critical assets, assessing the likelihood of various threats, and understanding their potential impact on the organization. Once risks are assessed, security policies should be crafted to provide clear guidelines on how to prevent, detect, and respond to incidents. These policies should articulate roles and responsibilities, outline approved procedures, and define the use of technology and tools for monitoring and incident management. A well-documented policy not only guides response efforts but also serves as an essential framework for ongoing security improvements.

The importance of training personnel cannot be understated when it comes to effectively responding to security incidents. Training should extend beyond theoretical knowledge to include practical, scenario-based exercises that prepare staff for real-world challenges. Employees at all levels must understand their role in the security framework, including recognizing security threats and understanding the protocols for reporting incidents. Regular drills and simulations can enhance this preparedness, providing valuable hands-on experience and revealing gaps in the response plan. Furthermore, fostering a culture of security awareness ensures that everyone is vigilant and capable of acting swiftly and correctly in the face of an incident. This collective readiness not only mitigates potential damage during an event but also reinforces the overall security posture of the organization.

Investing in both comprehensive policies and extensive training programs is essential. The balance between knowing how to navigate written procedures and the ability to react instinctively to changing situations can determine the effectiveness of an incident response. Regular reviews of both policies and training curricula are also necessary to adapt to the evolving threat landscape and to incorporate lessons learned from past incidents. By continuously refining these elements, organizations can greatly enhance their resilience and ensure that they are not only prepared to respond to incidents but also to prevent them wherever possible.

7.2 Detecting and Analyzing Incidents

Present methods for detecting incidents focus heavily on continuous monitoring and alerting mechanisms that are essential in today's cybersecurity landscape. Security operations center's (SOCs) implement advanced tools that enable real-time surveillance of network activity, endpoints, and data flows. By leveraging security information and event management (SIEM) systems and integrated threat detection solutions, organizations can cultivate a proactive posture. These systems aggregate logs and events from various sources to provide a comprehensive view of the environment. Analytical algorithms, machine learning models, and predefined rule sets are employed within these systems to automatically identify anomalous patterns indicating potential incidents. Effective alerting mechanisms prioritize threats based on established criteria, allowing security teams to focus on the most pressing issues while minimizing alert fatigue. Continuous tuning and updates to these monitoring tools enhance their effectiveness, ensuring they adapt to the evolving threat landscape.

Analyzing incidents involves a systematic approach to understanding the nature and impact of security events. Once an incident is detected, forensic analysis plays a critical role in delineating its scope and origin. Security analysts utilize techniques such as network traffic analysis, log examination, and endpoint reviews to construct a timeline of the incident. It is essential to identify the attack vector, the data affected, and the potential implications for the organization. By employing methodologies such as the Cyber Kill Chain or the MITRE ATT&CK framework, professionals can dissect incidents into phases, allowing for targeted responses. Collaborative investigations across teams can yield deeper insights into attacker behaviour, enabling a richer understanding of risks. Additionally, leveraging threat intelligence allows teams to correlate incidents with known threats, providing context that can lead to more informed decision-making.

Ultimately, building a robust incident detection and analysis capability requires an ongoing commitment to refinement and learning. Regularly updating detection mechanisms based on the latest threat intelligence, engaging in threat-hunting exercises, and participating in post-incident reviews can provide valuable insights that enhance future readiness. For organizations aiming to bolster their cybersecurity posture, integrating a combination of technology, analytics, and human expertise is vital. Furthermore, ensuring that all team members are trained in incident response protocols and analytical techniques enhances not only their confidence but also the overall effectiveness of the security operations.

7.3 Responding and Recovering from Incidents

When an incident occurs, having a clear response procedure is crucial to mitigate damage. This begins with containment strategies that aim to isolate the threat and prevent further spread. Effective containment strategies can include isolating affected systems from the network, disabling user accounts that show suspicious behaviour, and applying patches if vulnerabilities are being exploited. Excellent communication is equally important during incidents. All stakeholders, from technical teams to executive management, should be kept informed about the status of the incident, the implications of potential compromises, and the actions being taken. A well-documented communication plan can help ensure that everyone is on the same page and can aid in swift decision-making.

After immediate containment efforts, recovery processes must take center stage to restore systems to normal operations. This involves assessing the damage, identifying the root cause of the incident, and ensuring that systems are secure before being brought back online. In many cases, data restoration from secure backups is necessary to recover lost or compromised information. Consistent monitoring following an incident is essential to ensure that no remnants of the threat remain and that systems are stable. Additionally, debriefing sessions with all involved teams can extract valuable lessons learned, informing future incident response planning and enhancing the organization's overall security posture.

Having a practice run of both incident response and recovery processes through simulated cyber-attack exercises can greatly enhance a security team's readiness. These drills help ensure that all personnel are familiar with their roles and responsibilities, allowing for a more coordinated and effective response when a real incident occurs. Regular updates to the incident response plan, based on past experiences and emerging threats, can significantly improve both responsiveness and recovery efforts.

Chapter 8: Digital Forensics in Cyber Security

8.1 Introduction to Digital Forensics

Digital forensics is a specialized field that focuses on the recovery, analysis, and presentation of data from digital devices, networks, and storage systems after cyber incidents or breaches have occurred. Its primary role in investigating cyber incidents is to uncover evidence that demonstrates how a breach happened, identifies the perpetrators, and helps mitigate the impact of the incident. By utilizing various techniques to analyze digital footprints, forensic experts are able to recapture lost or deleted files, analyze communication logs, and examine malware footprints. This process not only helps in understanding the incident but also plays a crucial role in preventing future occurrences by identifying vulnerabilities within an organization's security infrastructure.

Maintaining evidence integrity during forensic investigations is paramount to ensuring that any findings can withstand legal scrutiny. Evidence collected in a digital forensic investigation must remain unaltered and preserved to maintain its authenticity and credibility. This includes employing proper chain-of-custody procedures, where every individual who handles the evidence documents their interaction with it. Techniques like using write blockers prevent any changes to the original data during the imaging process. When evidence is handled correctly, it strengthens the case in legal proceedings and allows for actionable insights that can improve an organization's security posture.

Keeping detailed logs and documentation throughout the entire forensic process not only protects the integrity of the evidence but also provides a roadmap should the need for further investigation arise in the future. These practices should be universally adopted by Security Operations, Incident Response teams, and third-party suppliers to ensure a high level of reliability and trustworthiness in digital forensic investigations.

8.2 Forensic Techniques and Tools

Forensic techniques play a crucial role in understanding and addressing cyber incidents. Data recovery and analysis are foundational to digital forensics, as they allow investigators to retrieve deleted or altered files that may hold vital clues. The process of data recovery can involve several methodologies, such as file carving, which is used to reconstruct files from unallocated space on a hard drive. Analyzing digital artifacts, such as metadata and logs, is also essential. Metadata can reveal when a file was created or modified, while log files can provide timelines of user activity and system changes. Understanding these aspects helps forensic experts to piece together the activities leading to a security incident, identifying when a breach occurred and how it happened.

In the realm of digital forensics, various tools have been developed to assist professionals in their investigations. Commonly used forensic tools include EnCase, FTK Imager, and Autopsy, which facilitate everything from disk imaging to file analysis. EnCase, for instance, is renowned for its powerful capabilities in evidence collection and reporting, helping forensic analysts create comprehensive documentation of their findings. FTK Imager allows for efficient data acquisition and creating forensic images of hard drives without modifying the original evidence, ensuring chain of custody is maintained. Autopsy, on the other hand, provides a user-friendly web interface for analysis, making it accessible even to those who may not have deep technical expertise. Each of these tools plays a specific role in an investigator's toolkit, and their applications can vary depending on the nature of the incident being investigated.

Utilizing the right forensic techniques and tools is vital for effective incident response. Incorporating proper methodologies for data analysis not only helps in uncovering the facts behind cyber incidents but also aids in future prevention efforts. One practical tip for security teams is to develop a clear forensic plan that details the procedures for evidence collection and analysis. This preparedness can significantly enhance efficiency during an incident response, ensuring that crucial evidence is not overlooked or mishandled.

8.3 Legal Considerations in Digital Forensics

The legal framework surrounding digital forensics is complex and vital for the validity of forensic investigations. Various laws regulate how evidence is collected, preserved, and presented in court. Forensic professionals must navigate legislation such as the Fourth Amendment in the United States, which protects citizens against unreasonable searches and seizures. This means that digital evidence should only be obtained with consent, through a warrant, or under exigent circumstances. Furthermore, the admissibility of digital evidence is governed by rules of evidence that vary by jurisdiction, such as the Federal Rules of Evidence in the U.S. These rules outline the necessity for authenticity, relevance, and lack of prejudice when presenting digital evidence in legal settings. Consequently, forensic experts must maintain rigorous chains of custody and develop meticulous documentation to ensure that evidence is not just collected legally, but is also prepared for scrutiny in a courtroom.

Compliance with regulations during forensic investigations is not merely a legal obligation but a cornerstone of the digital forensics discipline. There exist multiple standards and practices, such as those set by the National Institute of Standards and Technology (NIST) and the International Organization for Standardization (ISO), that outline how to conduct thorough and lawful forensic examinations. Adhering to these regulations helps ensure that the evidence collected is credible and defensible in legal proceedings. Moreover, organizations must be aware of privacy laws, such as the General Data Protection Regulation (GDPR) in the European Union, which dictate how personal data must be handled. Violating these regulations can result in severe penalties, including fines and reputational damage. Therefore, it is crucial for security operations teams to integrate legal knowledge into their incident response protocols, ensuring that any investigative measures taken not only meet security requirements but also align with legal standards.

Integrating legal considerations into the processes of digital forensics can offer organizations protection and enhance the credibility of their findings. Keeping up-to-date with evolving laws and best practices should be a constant endeavour for all professionals involved in incident response. This ensures that, when faced with the complexities of digital evidence, they are well-prepared to act within legal frameworks, thereby upholding both the integrity of the investigation and the organization's reputation.

Chapter 9: Compliance and Regulatory Frameworks

9.1 Overview of Cyber Security Regulations

Cyber security regulations are crucial for today's organizations, impacting how they protect sensitive data and maintain user privacy. Two prominent regulations are PCI-DSS and COPPA. The Payment Card Industry Data Security Standard (PCI-DSS) mandates that businesses handling payment card information follow stringent guidelines to safeguard cardholder data. This includes measures such as strong access control, maintaining a secure network, and regular monitoring of all access to network resources. On the other hand, the Children's Online Privacy Protection Act (COPPA) focuses on protecting the privacy of children under 13. It requires websites and online services directed at children to obtain verifiable parental consent before collecting personal information from young users. Understanding these regulations is essential for organizations as non-compliance can lead to severe penalties and reputational damage.

Regulatory compliance plays a vital role in enhancing an organization's security posture. By adhering to these regulations, organizations are often compelled to adopt best practices in their security frameworks, which helps mitigate risks associated with data breaches and cyber threats. Compliance initiatives typically include conducting regular audits, ensuring staff is trained on security protocols, and implementing advanced technology solutions for threat detection and incident response. Embracing a culture of compliance not only helps in meeting legal requirements but also fosters a proactive approach to security, thereby building trust among clients and stakeholders. Organizations often find that a robust compliance strategy serves as a foundation for broader security initiatives, creating an environment that deters cyber incidents while enabling effective incident management.

Staying ahead in compliance requires continuous education and adaptation as regulations evolve. Engaging with professional consultants and participating in industry forums can provide valuable insights into emerging requirements and proactive compliance strategies. Regularly updating security measures and ensuring that all teams, from incident response to third-party suppliers, are aligned with current regulations can greatly enhance an organization's resilience against cyber threats.

9.2 Compliance Standards (e.g., GDPR, HIPAA)

Compliance standards such as the General Data Protection Regulation (GDPR) and the Health Insurance Portability and Accountability Act (HIPAA) are designed to protect sensitive data and uphold privacy rights. The GDPR, which applies to organizations handling personal data of EU citizens, emphasizes transparency, consent, and individuals' rights over their data. It sets strict guidelines on how organizations must collect, store, and process personal information. Key requirements include obtaining explicit consent for data processing, enabling individuals to access their data, and ensuring a right to be forgotten. Similarly, HIPAA, which governs the healthcare industry in the United States, mandates that healthcare providers, payers, and their business associates safeguard sensitive patient information. HIPAA predefines operational standards for privacy, security, and breach notification to ensure that sensitive health records are securely handled and protected from unauthorized access.

When organizations fail to comply with these standards, the repercussions can be severe, ranging from hefty fines to reputational damage that can last for years. Non-compliance with GDPR can result in fines of up to 4% of annual global turnover or €20 million, whichever is greater. Beyond financial penalties, organizations may face legal actions from affected individuals or groups, which can lead to extensive litigation costs and even more reputational harm. For HIPAA, violations can attract penalties of up to $50,000 per incident, with a maximum annual penalty of $1.5 million. These consequences can disrupt operations significantly, leading to decreased consumer trust and loss of business opportunities. In a world where consumer confidence is paramount, organizations must treat compliance as a fundamental aspect of their operational integrity.

Ensuring compliance goes beyond just adhering to legal requirements; it enhances an organization's overall security posture. To avoid compliance pitfalls, companies should consider conducting regular risk assessments, implementing robust data protection measures, and establishing comprehensive training programs for their staff on compliance protocols and data security. Organizations must adopt a proactive approach to stay ahead of evolving regulations and threats, ensuring both data integrity and compliance are maintained. By fostering a culture of compliance, organizations not only avoid penalties but also build customer loyalty and trust, positioning themselves favourably in an increasingly competitive landscape.

9.3 Risk Management and Compliance Strategies

Understanding the intricate relationship between risk management strategies and compliance requirements in the realm of cybersecurity is essential for organizations of all sizes. Effective risk management goes beyond merely identifying potential threats; it incorporates a framework that ensures compliance with the various laws and regulations that govern data protection, privacy, and security practices. Organizations must first assess their unique risk landscape, which involves identifying assets, evaluating vulnerabilities, and understanding the potential impact of security incidents. Risk management frameworks like NIST, ISO 27001, and CIS controls can be aligned with compliance mandates such as GDPR, HIPAA, and PCI-DSS. This alignment helps create a comprehensive risk management strategy that not only safeguards an organization's assets but also adheres to regulatory requirements. Documented risk assessments and the implementation of mitigation measures are paramount, as they provide a clear audit trail that demonstrates compliance and readiness in the event of an incident.

Maintaining compliance in an ever-evolving regulatory landscape requires a proactive approach and an understanding of the shifting landscape of cybersecurity laws and standards. Continuous monitoring and adjustment of security practices are necessary to remain compliant as new regulations come into effect. Best practices include implementing a robust policy management system that emphasizes regular reviews and updates of security policies to align with compliance requirements. Additionally, training and education of personnel about the importance of compliance and their roles in maintaining it are crucial. Organizations should leverage automation tools for compliance checklists and reporting, which can streamline the process and reduce the risk of human error. Engaging with industry experts and participating in relevant forums or working groups can also help keep organizations informed about upcoming regulatory changes and best practices. Building a culture that prioritizes compliance, along with transparency and accountability, will aid organizations in navigating through the complexities of cybersecurity regulations effectively.

A practical tip for security teams is to establish regular communication with compliance officers and legal advisors. This collaboration ensures that cybersecurity strategies and compliance efforts are aligned, allowing for quicker responses to regulatory changes and reducing the risk of non-compliance. By fostering this partnership, organizations can better anticipate compliance challenges and develop more effective risk management strategies.

Chapter 10: Threat Hunting Strategies

10.1 Definition and Importance of Threat Hunting

Threat hunting is a proactive security practice that focuses on actively searching for undetected threats within an organization's environment. Unlike traditional security measures that rely on automated tools to identify and address known threats, threat hunting embodies a more audacious approach. Security professionals take the initiative to delve into the data and network activities, utilizing their expertise to uncover hidden anomalies that could indicate malicious activities. This hands-on engagement allows hunters to not only detect existing threats but also understand their behaviour, which is crucial for preventing future attacks.

The value of threat hunting lies in its ability to enhance traditional security measures. While conventional methods like firewalls, antivirus software, and intrusion detection systems provide foundational protection, they often fail to catch sophisticated, evolving threats that can evade automated tools. Threat hunters play a vital role in supplementing these defenses by using their intuition and analytical skills to spot signs of compromise. By identifying threats early in the kill chain, organizations can mitigate risks before they escalate into significant breaches. The integration of threat hunting into an organization's security strategy fosters a culture of vigilance and continuous improvement, empowering teams to adapt and respond effectively to the ever-changing threat landscape.

Incorporating threat hunting into your security operations can be greatly beneficial. It not only enhances your detection capabilities but also opens up invaluable insights into your network's vulnerabilities and potential attack vectors. Security Operations Center's (SOCs) equipped with a robust threat hunting capability can better prioritize their resources and tailor their defense strategies based on real-time intelligence. As a practical tip, consider establishing a dedicated threat hunting team within your SOC to ensure ongoing vigilance and proactive response, using threat intelligence as a foundation for their hunting activities.

10.2 Threat Hunting Methodologies

Common methodologies employed in threat hunting include hypothesis-driven and intelligence-led hunting. Hypothesis-driven hunting begins with an assumption about potential threats, allowing security professionals to test specific theories against existing data. This approach encourages structured thinking, as hunters formulate theories based on past incidents, observed behaviours, or emerging threat intelligence. The goal here is to validate or refute the hypotheses through careful analysis of logs, network traffic, and endpoints. On the other hand, intelligence-led hunting relies heavily on information gathered from various external sources, such as threat intelligence reports, industry news, or activity from known adversaries. By leveraging this information, security teams can actively search for signs of malicious activity that correlate with the threat landscape, focusing their efforts on high-risk areas that have been identified through intelligence. Both methodologies serve to enhance overall threat detection capabilities by fine-tuning the focus and approach of security analyses, ensuring that hunting efforts are not only reactive but as proactive as possible.

The iterative nature of threat hunting plays a crucial role in the continuous improvement of security practices. This iterative process consists of a cycle of hunting, detecting, learning, and adapting, where each hunt provides insights that feed back into the next. After each round of hunting, findings should be meticulously documented and analyzed to refine existing models, develop new hypotheses, and understand the attack methods used by adversaries. This feedback loop fosters an environment of learning and adaptation within security teams. As threats evolve, so too do the techniques and tactics employed during hunts. Security operations become more resilient as the experience from prior hunts informs future strategies, making practices increasingly robust over time. This assurance not only enhances the team's capabilities but also builds a deeper understanding of the organization's unique threat profile, allowing for more tailored and effective defenses.

For security professionals, one practical tip is to ensure that insights gained from threat hunting are shared across the organization. Collaborating with other teams and departments can enhance situational awareness and provide additional context to the activities being monitored. By fostering an open dialogue about threat hunting findings, teams can work together to improve overall security posture and better prepare for future incidents.

10.3 Tools and Resources for Threat Hunting

Identifying the right tools and resources is crucial for effective threat hunting. Organizations have access to a variety of analytics platforms that can help in detecting and analyzing potential threats. These analytics platforms often leverage advanced machine learning algorithms to sift through vast amounts of data, identifying anomalies that could signify malicious activities. Furthermore, threat intelligence sources play a key role in providing context to these findings. They offer insights into known threats, vulnerabilities, and attack patterns that cyber adversaries may employ. Well-known threat intelligence platforms, such as Recorded Future or Threat Connect, aggregate data from numerous sources, helping teams stay ahead of evolving threats. Security Information and Event Management (SIEM) systems also stand out as essential tools; they gather data from across the network, enabling real-time visibility and incident response capabilities. Investing in these resources allows security operations teams to enhance their threat detection capabilities efficiently.

Collaboration and community engagement significantly bolster threat hunting efforts. Cyber threats are not confined to one organization; they affect entire industries, making information sharing vital. By engaging with the security community, teams can share experiences, tactics, and insights that may help identify new threats faster. Initiatives such as Information Sharing and Analysis Center's (ISACs) encourage organizations to collaborate and share threat intelligence. This collaborative approach not only strengthens an organization's defensive posture but also fosters a sense of unity in the fight against cybercrime. Engaging with external vendors and third-party suppliers can also provide additional resources and expertise, creating a more robust security environment. Remember, the more knowledge is shared across the community, the better equipped all organizations will be in the ongoing battle against sophisticated threats.

Understanding the landscape of tools and fostering a collaborative environment are fundamental to proactive threat hunting. Continuous research into emerging tools can offer new solutions to evolving threats, while participating in community discussions ensures that security strategies remain relevant and effective. Always consider how relationships with peers and vendors can enhance your threat detection capabilities. A strong network combined with the right tools creates a formidable defense against cyber adversaries.

Chapter 11: Incident Response Plans and Policies

11.1 Developing an Incident Response Plan

To create an effective Incident Response Plan (IRP), it is essential to include key components that facilitate a structured response to security incidents. The first critical element is incident identification, which requires the clear definition of what constitutes an incident within the context of an organization. Detection mechanisms such as intrusion detection systems, security information and event management (SIEM) tools, and employee reporting must be incorporated to ensure swift identification. Following identification, escalation procedures should be meticulously outlined, detailing the steps to take as the incident severity increases. This includes establishing a chain of command and communication pathways that ensure the right people are informed and involved throughout the process. Moreover, documentation must be standardized, specifying how incidents will be logged, tracked, and analyzed. Such procedures allow for a quick and organized response, minimize damage, and facilitate post-incident reviews to improve future resilience.

Stakeholder involvement is of paramount importance when developing a comprehensive incident response plan. Engaging individuals from various departments—such as IT, legal, compliance, human resources, and public relations—ensures that all perspectives are considered, and responsibilities are clearly defined. This interdisciplinary collaboration fosters a culture of security awareness and generates buy-in from all stakeholders, promoting a more effective and cohesive response. Additionally, involving stakeholders in the planning process allows for the identification of unique vulnerabilities within different areas of the organization, leading to a more tailored approach to incident response. Ensuring that all relevant parties are part of simulated incident response drills or tabletop exercises further solidifies this approach, preparing the organization to respond swiftly and efficiently to real incidents.

Maintaining a living document that reflects the changing nature of threats and the organization itself is vital for an effective Incident Response Plan. Regular updates that incorporate lessons learned from previous incidents and adjustments to operational realities will ensure that the plan remains relevant and actionable. For organizations looking to build a robust IRP, continuous education and training of team members and stakeholders should be a priority. This proactive stance cultivates an adaptable and resilient cybersecurity posture that will enhance the overall effectiveness of incident response efforts.

11.2 Incident Response Policy Frameworks

Establishing a robust incident response policy framework is crucial for guiding organizations in their incident management efforts. These frameworks serve as structured guides that help organizations develop, implement, and maintain their incident response policies effectively. They provide a standardized approach to managing security incidents, ensuring consistency across the organization. Frameworks often incorporate best practices, legal and regulatory requirements, and lessons learned from previous incidents, enabling organizations to respond decisively to threats and minimize damage. By utilizing established frameworks, such as NIST's Computer Security Incident Handling Guide or ISO/IEC 27035, security teams can create incident response strategies that align with their specific operational needs and risk profiles. This allows for a clearer understanding of roles and responsibilities, enabling teams to act swiftly and efficiently in the face of an incident.

Regularly reviewing and updating incident response policies is not just a best practice; it is a necessity in an ever-evolving threat landscape. Organizations must adapt their policies to reflect the changing nature of threats, technological advancements, and evolving business processes. Cyber threats grow more sophisticated day by day, often exploiting gaps in outdated policies. A regular review cycle ensures that the incident response plan remains relevant and effective. It also provides an opportunity to incorporate insights gained from recent incidents, tabletop exercises, and threat intelligence reports. Engaging stakeholders across the organization during these reviews fosters a culture of security awareness and prepares teams for real-world scenarios. Ultimately, by keeping incident response policies current, organizations enhance their resilience and ability to mitigate impacts when incidents occur.

One practical tip for maintaining effective incident response policies is to establish a formal review schedule, integrating it with other critical operational assessments within the organization. By doing so, you create a systematic approach that encourages teams to regularly evaluate their procedures and learn from past experiences without waiting for a significant incident to occur. This proactive stance is integral to developing a mature incident response capability.

11.3 Training and Simulation for Incident Response

Training programs are crucial in preparing personnel for incident response roles. When a cyber incident occurs, having well-trained staff can mean the difference between a swift resolution and a prolonged crisis. Effective training ensures that all team members understand their responsibilities, procedures, and the tools at their disposal. Comprehensive programs should cover various scenarios, including both common and sophisticated attacks, to ensure that personnel can respond effectively under pressure. Regularly scheduled training helps to not only refresh skills but also adapt to evolving threats in the cybersecurity landscape. Moreover, fostering a culture of continuous improvement and learning within an organization can empower response teams to become more effective and confident in handling incidents.

The role of simulations and tabletop exercises is pivotal in testing incident response plans. Simulations create realistic scenarios that allow teams to practice their response strategies in a controlled environment. These exercises can reveal gaps in the existing plans, highlight areas needing improvement, and test the coordination between different response teams and external partners. Tabletop exercises, in particular, provide an opportunity for personnel to discuss their roles in hypothetical situations, enhancing communication and collaboration. Through these exercises, organizations can evaluate their readiness to act efficiently during a real incident and adjust their strategies accordingly. Engaging in regular simulations is not just about testing the plan; it is about honing skills and ensuring that all team members are aligned and able to perform effectively when it truly matters.

Developing a robust training and simulation program is vital for any organization aiming to strengthen its incident response capabilities. This proactive approach not only builds team confidence but also enhances the overall resilience of the organization against cyber threats. Ensuring that personnel are prepared to deal with incidents can significantly reduce the time to detect and respond to breaches, ultimately protecting vital assets and maintaining stakeholder trust.

Chapter 12: Cyber Security Metrics and Reporting

12.1 Measuring Security Performance

Measuring security performance in an organization involves utilizing various metrics that can provide insights into the effectiveness of security measures and protocols. Key performance indicators (KPIs) such as incident response times, the number of detected threats, incident closure rates, and user compliance levels serve as essential tools for evaluating an organization's security posture. Other important metrics can include the mean time to detect (MTTD) and mean time to respond (MTTR) to incidents, which help quantify the speed and efficiency of the security operations. Organizations may also measure the volume and types of security incidents over time, enabling them to identify patterns and trends that require attention. By systematically tracking these metrics, security teams can ascertain how well security policies function in real scenarios, facilitating a climate of ongoing improvement and proactive adjustments.

Continuous measurement plays a pivotal role in informing security strategy adjustments and enhancements. As threat landscapes evolve, real-time data collected through various security tools allows organizations to adapt quickly. Regularly assessing the effectiveness of current measures reveals whether existing controls are still adequate or if modifications are necessary to mitigate new and emerging risks. For instance, if the frequency of ransomware attacks rises within a particular sector, organizations may need to become more vigilant in monitoring for signs of compromise and invest in employee training around phishing tactics. This iterative process of measurement and adjustment not only fortifies an organization's security posture but also fosters a culture of resilience. Continuous feedback loops ensure that strategies are agile, allowing security operations center's to rapidly pivot in response to shifting threats.

Establishing benchmarks based on these metrics is crucial. Organizations should not only focus on the collected data but also on how they compare to industry standards or peer organizations. This benchmarking can illuminate gaps in security practices and pinpoint areas needing further investment. A practical tip would be to implement regular security performance reviews that include diverse stakeholders—security architects, incident response teams, and even upper management—to ensure a holistic view of the security strategy. These reviews should assess whether the metrics align with the organization's overarching goals, driving optimal security and operational efficiency.

12.2 Key Performance Indicators (KPIs) for SOC

Identifying key performance indicators relevant to the effectiveness of Security Operations Center's (SOCs) is crucial for measuring their success in defending an organization against threats. Some of the most critical KPIs include the mean time to detect (MTTD) incidents, mean time to respond (MTTR) to incidents, and the number of incidents detected versus the number of incidents escalated. MTTD focuses on the average duration taken to identify security threats, highlighting the SOC's capability to recognize issues before they escalate.

Conversely, MTTR emphasizes how quickly the SOC can respond and manage these incidents after detection. Both metrics are essential in evaluating the operational efficiency of SOC teams. Furthermore, the ratio of incidents escalated provides insights into the SOC's prioritization processes and can indicate the effectiveness of the initial detection practices. Regularly assessing these KPIs allows organizations to understand their security posture and the areas that require enhancement.

The exploration of KPIs facilitates performance assessment and operational improvements by providing quantitative data that can be analyzed over time. This analysis enables SOC teams to identify trends, recognize patterns in incident occurrences, and establish benchmarks that guide operational strategies. Monitoring these indicators aids in optimizing resource allocation, training requirements, and technology investments. Additionally, KPIs can be correlated with threat intelligence to improve predictive capabilities, allowing teams to prepare for potential risks. By continuously evaluating and adjusting based on KPI insights, organizations can enhance their security measures, reduce response times, and ultimately improve the overall readiness of their SOC. This data-driven approach fosters a culture of continuous improvement within the Security Operations framework, making it essential for any organization serious about its cybersecurity efforts.

Establishing a routine for KPI tracking and reporting can yield significant benefits. Organizations should consider integrating KPI dashboards that provide real-time insights into their SOC's performance. By fostering a transparent environment where data is readily available, teams can engage in more informed discussions about security challenges and collaborative problem-solving. Whether through regular review meetings or automated reports, sharing performance outcomes encourages accountability and motivates teams to achieve their goals. Prioritizing KPIs not only enhances tactical operations but also supports strategic planning and alignment with broader business objectives.

12.3 Reporting Incident Metrics to Stakeholders

When reporting incident metrics to stakeholders, it is vital to focus on clarity and relevance. Metrics should be presented in a way that highlights their impact on the organization and helps stakeholders understand their significance. This means using straightforward language and avoiding technical jargon that might confuse those not directly involved in cybersecurity. Providing visual aids like charts and graphs can also enhance understanding, as they offer a quick snapshot of the data that can make trends and patterns more recognizable. It's essential to tailor the report to the audience at hand; for instance, executive summaries should focus on high-level insights, while operational teams may require deeper technical details. In addition, metric selection is crucial—focusing on key performance indicators (KPIs) that align with the organization's goals ensures that the report addresses what truly matters to the stakeholders. This could involve metrics such as time to detect, time to respond, and the overall impact on business continuity. By prioritizing relevant metrics and presenting them clearly, you facilitate informed decision-making and encourage stakeholder engagement.

Transparency and communication form the bedrock of trust between security operations teams and stakeholders. Being open about security incidents, the metrics surrounding them, and the response efforts fosters a culture of accountability. Regular updates, even when incidents are minor or when no incidents have occurred, demonstrate vigilance and commitment to security. This proactive communication can counteract potential negativity or misunderstanding stemming from silence or delayed information. Engaging stakeholders in dialogue further strengthens this relationship. By inviting feedback on reports or conducting review sessions, you encourage an interactive environment where stakeholders feel their insights are valued. This collaborative approach not only boosts trust but also enhances the overall effectiveness of the incident response process. Always remember that creating clear channels of communication and being transparent in reporting ensures that stakeholders feel informed and involved, cultivating an atmosphere of confidence in the organization's cybersecurity initiatives.

When disseminating incident metrics, be prepared to adapt your reporting style based on the feedback received from stakeholders. Regularly ask for input regarding the format and content of the reports to ensure they remain effective and relevant over time. This commitment to improving communication can greatly enhance the relationship between your cybersecurity team and stakeholders, leading to more effective incident management and an overall stronger security posture.

Chapter 13: Advanced Persistent Threats (APTs)

13.1 Understanding APTs

Advanced Persistent Threats (APTs) are a category of cyber threats characterized by their sophisticated and organized nature. Unlike typical cyber threats that might be opportunistic and often short-lived, APTs are typically methodical, continual, and aimed at gaining access to sensitive information over extended periods. APTs involve a combination of various tactics, techniques, and procedures (TTPs) that can adapt over time, allowing the attacker to stay undetected while pursuing their ultimate objectives. These threats are not merely one-off attacks; they feature phases of infiltration, lateral movement, data exfiltration, and often persistence within the target network. This distinguishes them from other cyber threats such as ransomware or denial-of-service attacks that are usually more transactional and demand immediate results.

The motivations behind APT attacks are often aligned with strategic interests, whether they be economic, political, or military. State-sponsored actors frequently employ APTs to conduct espionage, seeking valuable intelligence and data that could give them a competitive edge. Private organizations may also become targets, particularly if they hold trade secrets or proprietary information. Additionally, critical infrastructure, financial institutions, and governmental agencies are prominent targets for APTs due to the nature of their operations and the sensitive information they handle. The long-term investment by threat actors in APT campaigns indicates a desire for sustained access rather than a quick payoff, underscoring the serious implications for organizations that may find themselves under siege.

Security teams must recognize the unique qualities of APTs to effectively counter them. Understanding their multi-phase attack structure can help in developing a comprehensive security posture that addresses the prevention, detection, and response aspects. Moreover, enhancing the organization's threat intelligence capabilities is crucial, as it allows for early identification of potential indicators of compromise, giving teams a timely advantage in thwarting these protracted and complex threats. Regularly updating incident response plans and training personnel to recognize the subtle signs of APT activity can significantly elevate an organization's resilience against these advanced threats.

13.2 Detection and Mitigation Strategies for APTs

Organizations today face an unprecedented threat landscape, with Advanced Persistent Threats (APTs) representing one of the most insidious and long-lasting dangers. To effectively detect APTs, organizations must adopt a multifaceted approach that incorporates a combination of continuous monitoring, threat intelligence, and behavioural analysis. One key methodology is the use of a Security Information and Event Management (SIEM) system, which aggregates and correlates data from various sources to identify anomalous behaviour indicative of a potential APT. Integrating threat intelligence feeds into the SIEM can enhance the detection capabilities, allowing analysts to recognize indicators of compromise (IOCs) that align with known APT campaigns. In addition, leveraging user and entity behaviour analytics (UEBA) can help in spotting deviations from normal user activity that might suggest account compromise or insider threats. Regular vulnerability assessments and penetration testing also play crucial roles in fortifying defenses and uncovering potential entry points that APT actors might exploit.

When a potential APT is detected, containment and response strategies become critical for mitigating damage and preventing further compromise. One effective strategy involves implementing a designated incident response plan tailored specifically for APT scenarios. This plan should outline clear roles and responsibilities, ensuring that every member of the incident response team knows their tasks during an incident. Establishing network segmentation can also limit the lateral movement of APT actors within the infrastructure, minimizing their ability to reach sensitive data. Engaging in proactive threat hunting can help identify APT indicators that may have evaded detection. Furthermore, ensuring that endpoint detection and response (EDR) solutions are deployed can provide real-time visibility into endpoint activities, enabling quicker identification and isolation of compromised systems. Post-incident, it is vital to analyze and document the incident to derive lessons learned and update defenses accordingly, enhancing the organization's resilience against future APT attempts.

Prioritizing a culture of security awareness is another effective tactic in both detection and response strategies. Training employees on recognizing phishing attempts and other threats can reduce the likelihood of successful APT infiltration. Regularly updating and patching systems to close known vulnerabilities is essential, as APT actors often exploit outdated software. Collaborating with external security partners for penetration testing and threat assessments can provide additional insights into potential weaknesses. For maximum effectiveness, it's essential to maintain an agile security posture, adapting quickly to evolving threats and continuously refining detection and response capabilities based on the latest intelligence and best practices.

13.3 Case Studies of APT Incidents

Throughout recent history, several Advanced Persistent Threat (APT) incidents have underscored the complex nature of cybersecurity threats. One notable case is the 2010 Stuxnet attack, which targeted Iran's nuclear facilities. This sophisticated worm not only infected industrial control systems but also caused physical damage by manipulating machinery. The attackers demonstrated a level of sophistication that included extensive knowledge of their target's infrastructure, highlighting the need for organizations to understand their critical systems and the threats they face. Another significant example is the 2014 breach of Sony Pictures, attributed to a group calling itself the Guardians of Peace. This incident resulted in the exfiltration of sensitive corporate data and disrupted operations, revealing how APT groups can effectively utilize social engineering alongside malware to achieve their objectives. The methods employed in these and other APT incidents often involve multi-faceted approaches, including initial reconnaissance, exploitation of vulnerabilities, and maintenance of persistence within the network, all of which can have devastating consequences for organizations.

Learning from these incidents is crucial for improving security practices. For instance, organizations can derive several lessons from the Stuxnet attack, particularly the importance of securing not just IT systems but also operational technology. Understanding the intricacies of the environment can lead to better defenses against tailored threats. Additionally, the Sony Pictures hack emphasizes the need for robust incident response plans and the importance of training employees to recognize phishing attempts, which are often the entry points for these attacks. Regular security assessments, timely patch management, and comprehensive employee education about social engineering tactics can significantly bolster an organization's resilience against APTs. Furthermore, cultivating a strong collaboration among security operations teams and continuous threat intelligence sharing can foster a proactive defense posture, ensuring that organizations are not just reacting to incidents but anticipating them.

Ultimately, adopting a multi-layered security strategy that accounts for the evolving tactics of APT groups can lay a strong foundation for future cybersecurity efforts. Security teams should focus on enhancing visibility within their environments and implementing effective detection mechanisms. Regularly reviewing and updating incident response plans in light of new intelligence can also ensure readiness for potential threats. In a landscape where APT tactics continue to evolve, staying informed and adaptable can prevent organizations from becoming the next target.

Chapter 14: Vendor and Third-party Risk Management

14.1 Assessing Third-party Cyber Risks

Assessing the cyber risks linked to third-party vendors requires a comprehensive understanding of various methodologies employed to evaluate and manage these risks. Organizations should start by conducting a thorough risk assessment that encompasses the vendor's security policies, practices, and historical data breaches, if any. Engaging in a detailed questionnaire can help gauge a vendor's security posture, examining factors such as employee training, data handling policies, and incident response plans. Additionally, leveraging industry frameworks like NIST or ISO standards provides a structured approach for evaluation, ensuring consistent and thorough analysis. Risk assessments should also include the evaluation of physical security measures, regulatory compliance, and the vendor's overall reputation in the market. An effective assessment integrates qualitative and quantitative models to establish risk ratings that can aid in decision-making regarding vendor relationships.

The importance of continuous monitoring of third-party vendors cannot be overstated. Cyber threats are evolving rapidly, and a vendor's compliance and security posture may change unexpectedly. Maintaining a dynamic risk management strategy necessitates ongoing oversight of a vendor's security controls, incident reports, and compliance certifications. Implementing tools for continuous monitoring, such as security ratings or threat intelligence feeds, equips organizations with real-time insights into the risk landscape surrounding their vendors. Regularly scheduled audits and assessments supplement automated monitoring efforts and reinforce accountability, ensuring that vendors uphold security practices and comply with agreed-upon standards. By continuously evaluating third-party engagements, organizations can mitigate potential vulnerabilities and respond proactively to emerging threats, fostering a secure supply chain environment.

To bolster the resilience of your organization against third-party risks, establish a clear communication plan with your vendors. Ensuring that both parties are aligned on security protocols and response plans can enhance your overall security posture. This proactive approach not only facilitates timely updates when risks arise but also promotes a culture of security awareness among all involved parties. Both parties must remember that effective risk management is a shared responsibility.

14.2 Frameworks for Vendor Security Assessment

When conducting thorough vendor security assessments, it is crucial to utilize established frameworks and benchmarks that provide a structured approach. Popular frameworks such as NIST Cybersecurity Framework, ISO 27001, and the CIS Critical Security Controls offer guidance in evaluating vendor risk and security posture. These frameworks help organizations define and implement required security measures, allowing them to assess how well a vendor's practices align with their own security needs. By applying these established guidelines, organizations can ensure comprehensive evaluations that address potential vulnerabilities in vendor systems and processes, helping to protect sensitive information and maintain regulatory compliance.

Establishing security criteria that align with an organization's objectives is essential for effective vendor assessments. Each organization has unique goals, risk appetites, and regulatory requirements that must be taken into account when defining these criteria. This alignment not only ensures that the security measures are relevant but also fosters a deeper understanding of the security challenges that third-party suppliers may face. It is important to consider factors such as data sensitivity, industry standards, and specific operational requirements when developing these security criteria. By doing so, organizations can tailor their assessments to better evaluate the security capabilities of their vendors and make informed decisions on partnerships.

To enhance the effectiveness of vendor security assessments, organizations should continually update their frameworks and criteria to reflect evolving cyber threats and changing business environments. Regularly reviewing and revising these standards can help keep pace with new vulnerabilities and technologies. Engaging in collaborative assessment processes with vendors can also provide valuable insights into their security practices and foster a culture of mutual responsibility towards safeguarding information. Regular engagement and clear communication can create a stronger overall security posture, benefiting both the organization and its third-party suppliers.

14.3 Incident Response Coordination with Third-party Vendors

Coordination between organizations and their vendors is essential during incident response situations. When a security incident occurs, the involvement of third-party suppliers can significantly impact the effectiveness and speed of the response. Vendors often have unique insights into their products or services, and their expertise can help organizations manage the incident more efficiently. This partnership is crucial because vendors may hold key information that can aid in identifying the root cause of an incident, as well as understanding potential vulnerabilities associated with their products. Without proper coordination and communication, organizations risk misunderstandings that can aggravate the situation, leading to prolonged downtimes and exacerbated damage. Ensuring that organizations have established protocols for working with vendors allows for a swift and comprehensive approach to mitigation, which is essential in today's threat landscape.

Effective incident response protocols must include clear lines of communication and a robust framework for information sharing. During a security incident, time is of the essence, and vendors should be informed promptly of incidents that may impact their services or products. Organizations can set up a dedicated communication channel to facilitate real-time updates. This can include secure messaging applications or incident response platforms that enable swift data sharing and collaboration between teams. Additionally, organizations should establish guidelines that outline what information can be shared, with whom, and at what stages of the incident lifecycle. This ensures that sensitive data is protected while still allowing for the flow of crucial information. Regular drills and tabletop exercises involving both internal teams and third-party vendors can enhance understanding and establish trust, ensuring everyone is on the same page during a real incident.

Implementation of a Third-party Vendor Risk Management Program is also beneficial. This program should assess the vendors' cybersecurity postures regularly, ensuring they comply with the organization's security standards. By conducting risk assessments, organizations can better understand potential vulnerabilities that could arise from their vendors. Furthermore, including clauses in vendor contracts that address incident response responsibilities will help formalize expectations and processes ahead of time, making it easier to navigate incidents as they arise. A well-structured coordination plan not only fortifies the organization's incident response capabilities but also strengthens relationships with vendors, fostering a collaborative environment geared toward mutual resilience against cyber threats.

Chapter 15: Future Trends in Cyber Security Operations

15.1 Emerging Threat Landscapes

Emerging threats in the cyber landscape are constantly evolving, driven by advancements in technology and shifts in socio-economic factors. One significant threat on the horizon is the rise of artificial intelligence and machine learning tools used by cybercriminals. These tools can automate attacks, analyze vulnerabilities in systems more efficiently, and enable personalized phishing schemes that are harder to detect. Additionally, the proliferation of Internet of Things (IoT) devices has created a larger attack surface, as many of these devices often lack robust security measures or timely updates. Ransomware remains a critical threat, with attackers adopting sophisticated tactics that include targeting specific industries to maximize their payouts. Moreover, the emergence of nation-state actors employing cyber tactics for espionage and disruption adds another layer of complexity, as these groups have substantial resources and capabilities at their disposal. Understanding these evolving threats is crucial for organizations aiming to bolster their cybersecurity posture and stay ahead of potential breaches.

To prepare for the ever-changing cyber threat landscape, organizations must adopt a proactive approach to cybersecurity. This begins with conducting regular risk assessments to identify vulnerabilities within their systems. Organizations should invest in up-to-date security technologies that leverage artificial intelligence for enhanced threat detection and response capabilities. Implementing a robust incident response plan is also essential, enabling quick action when a security breach occurs. Training employees on cybersecurity best practices is equally important, as human error remains a significant factor in many cyber incidents. Collaborating with third-party suppliers ensures a collective defense strategy that shares threat intelligence and cybersecurity insights, enhancing the security framework. Lastly, organizations should prioritize regular updates and patches to their software and systems, as this is one of the most effective ways to defend against known vulnerabilities. By staying informed and adaptable, businesses can better navigate the complexities of future cyber threats.

A practical tip for organizations is to implement a continuous monitoring strategy. This approach allows security teams to have real-time visibility into their network activities, helping them swiftly detect and respond to anomalous behaviour that might indicate an emerging threat.

15.2 Innovations in Cyber Security Technologies

Innovations in cyber security technologies are increasingly shaped by the advancements in artificial intelligence (AI), machine learning, and blockchain. AI and machine learning, in particular, empower security systems to adapt and evolve, enabling them to not only detect but also predict potential threats. By analyzing vast amounts of data, these technologies can identify patterns and anomalies that signify an attack. This proactive approach is crucial in today's landscape where cyber threats are growing more sophisticated and varied. Machine learning algorithms can improve over time, learning from new data to enhance their accuracy in identifying threats, thereby reducing the occurrence of false positives which can overwhelm security teams.

Blockchain presents another innovative avenue for enhancing cyber security. By utilizing decentralized ledgers, organizations can ensure higher levels of data integrity and transparency. This technology secures transactions in a way that is efficient and tamper-proof, making it challenging for malicious actors to alter records without detection. Furthermore, smart contracts can automate security protocols, enforcing consistent security policies without the need for central oversight. Together with AI and machine learning, blockchain creates a multi-layered security posture that provides resilience against breaches.

These innovations significantly enhance security operations and defenses. With AI-driven solutions, security operations center's (SOCs) can streamline incident detection and response processes. By automating routine tasks, SOC analysts can focus on more complex threats that require human judgment and expertise. The integration of machine learning allows for real-time threat intelligence, which can lead to quicker incident responses and improved threat containment strategies. Employing AI-based solutions also facilitates better resource allocation, ensuring that SOC teams can react promptly without being overwhelmed. Leveraging these innovative technologies is not just a competitive advantage; it is a necessary evolution in the fight against cyber threats. Security professionals must stay informed about these advancements and consider how they can be integrated into their existing frameworks for enhanced protection.

15.3 Preparing for the Future of Cyber Security Operations

Organizations must take strategic steps to future-proof their cyber security operations to address the rapidly evolving threat landscape. This begins with a thorough risk assessment to identify current vulnerabilities and potential future risks. By understanding the specific challenges they face, organizations can develop targeted security strategies that not only address immediate issues but also anticipate future threats. Implementing a zero-trust architecture is critical, where strict access controls are enforced, ensuring that every user, device, and application must be verified before gaining access to essential resources. Regularly updating and patching software and systems can minimize the risk posed by known vulnerabilities, while investing in advanced threat intelligence solutions can provide organizations with the necessary insights to predict and prepare for emerging attacks. Furthermore, establishing strong partnerships with third-party suppliers is vital, as these vendors are often at the forefront of security innovation and can aid organizations in enhancing their security posture.

The importance of adaptability and agility in responding to emerging threats cannot be overstated. As cyber threats become more sophisticated, organizations must be prepared to pivot quickly to mitigate potential damage. This requires not only flexible security protocols but also a culture of continuous learning and improvement within the security operations teams. Training exercises, including tabletop simulations and red team-blue team scenarios, help cultivate this agility by allowing teams to practice their response strategies in controlled environments. Additionally, leveraging automation in threat detection and incident response can streamline processes, enabling teams to react faster while reducing the chances of human error. By fostering a mindset that embraces change and encourages rapid problem-solving, organizations can position themselves to effectively navigate the complexities of cyber security in the future.

Collaboration plays a crucial role in building resilience against cyber threats. Organizations should not only focus on internal collaboration among teams such as incident response, SOC, and threat detection, but also engage in information sharing with external partners and industry peers. Participating in threat intelligence sharing communities can enhance an organization's situational awareness and provide real-time updates on evolving threats. Adopting a proactive approach to cyber security, which includes threat hunting and simulation of various attack scenarios, can further strengthen the defense mechanisms in place. A practical tip for organizations looking to future-proof their cyber security operations is to develop a comprehensive incident response plan that is regularly updated and tested. This ensures that all team members know their roles during a security incident, can act swiftly, and reduce the impact of any attacks.